Published By

Wold Meridian Press
Brockholes
Farlesthorpe Road
Alford
Lincolnshire
LN13 9PS
UK

© 2022 Alastair Lodge

No part of this book may be reproduced in any form or by any means, Electronic or mechanical, including photocopying and recording, or by any Information storage and retrieval system, including the internet, without written permission from the publisher or author.

All rights of performance and recording strictly reserved

Forward

This is a companion to my earlier volume **Chording to the Dance Masters** which presented 44 of my favourite Renaissance Dance band tunes and arranged them as a single melody line with chords derived from the original harmony lines. In the next two volumes I have reunited the melody line with the lower parts in the score, so that with more collaborators, the fullness of the original arrangement can be heard. The chords are still present, so if the ensemble is short handed, and lines are missing, the arrangements will still work. What is more, by contrasting the melody and chords with the full scoring, it should be possible to work some light and shade into performances.

Who were the Publishers and the Dance Masters? What did they do?

Some time around the 1500s, the popularity of dance music exploded in Europe. Dance Masters were collecting chansons and dance tunes from courts and rural parts and were teaching these to new audiences, spreading their arrangements and reflecting the performance styles of the areas from which they had collected the tunes. Publishers were able to take these tunes that were becoming known across the regions and nations and spread them even more widely, thanks to technological innovations in music printing which made it quicker and therefore cheaper to produce collections of these dances in four or more parts. These publishers were often highly accomplished composers in their own right, who were both able to provide distinctive harmony lines and compose new tunes in the style of their sources, feeding the courts with enduring tunes.

Composers and printers of this time would often use note values that are double the length of those we would be used to seeing today, and so to make this version more readable, breves have become semibreves or whole notes, semibreves have become minims or half notes and so on . At times bar lines have been shifted so that the metre makes more sense (No. 4 Schäfertanz Ohne Fels, is a case in point, originally printed with the bar lines suggesting 4/4 time whilst the melody stubbornly manifests 3 /4 time!).

As a supplement to this publication I have uploaded a playlist of the 44 pieces on to YouTube and this is available here:

https://youtube.com/playlist?list=PLYRWH2nycMkMoIoEYEMVPa_EXY6NVDpNS

The performances feature the version given here with the melody line accompanied with chords played by a harpsichord voice, and these are alternated with the original scoring in all its parts. I think these demonstrate that the chord arrangements are faithful to the original composer's arrangements. Please note that these are midi generated performances which lack the charm of real performances. Instrumentation has been restricted as few of the available voices sound at all authentic, and there is much that could be improved upon by your own efforts and with imaginative articulation. They do at least demonstrate how the chords work with the melody and I hope that they provide some inspiration and guidance for practice, and also that the contemporary artwork and historical information enhances the experience.

Working with this publication

For those just starting out in Early Music, the volume is an ideal introduction, since the ensemble can build from a soloist with accompaniment with the chords alone, and parts can be added in as additional musicians become available. Instrumentation for these pieces was not specified in the original prints. The range of each part is quite limited, and though the harmonies may seem strange at times, key signatures are kind to the less experienced musician. If enthusiasm takes hold then reproductions of early music instruments are sold by some very talented makers, as well as coming up on auction sites. Otherwise, it is possible to put together a fairly convincing ensemble with recorders, violins, a cello and mandolins, bouzoukis, flutes or guitars and gradually introduce the authentic instruments as they become available.

21/03/2023 New practice videos launched for learning harmony lines for this publication

We are pleased to announce newly added content on YouTube released for this volume: There are now separate videos for the Alto Tenor and Bass line for each piece which aim to make the process of playing the harmony lines even easier. These have been collected into playlists for the Alto, Tenor and Bass lines. For each part, the line in question can be heard first on its own, accompanied by the chords and percussion, and on the repeats with the addition of the melody line and on further repeat with the whole ensemble, although the other parts are reduced in volume in the mix so that the line to be learned is still identifiable.

Alto line playlist:
https://www.youtube.com/playlist?list=PLYRWH2nycMkNVDVUVp8y08eAdt5utNObA

Tenor line playlist:
https://www.youtube.com/playlist?list=PLYRWH2nycMkO4fUCoAGPf_BL0y5WklfqU

Bass line playlist
https://www.youtube.com/playlist?list=PLYRWH2nycMkMnBIzH5lKWs7MpZzVq1dxk

About the Editor

Alastair Lodge was bitten by the Early Music bug as a pre-teenager, through the inspiration of David Munrow and other pioneers of renaissance music in the 1970s. He began collecting Early Music recordings and mediaeval instruments at this time and formed an early music group with his friends who attended the Chester Cathedral Choir School. At first this group, The St Werburgh Consort, functioned with just recorders, a violin, cello and percussion, but was soon supplemented, so that by the time it played its final concerts, it boasted a cornamuse, crumhorn, kortholt, rackett, rauschpfeife, rebec, gittern and cornettino.

From there Alastair gained a Music Exhibition at Shrewsbury School where he founded the Sabrina Consort, playing early music at concerts around the town. At St Andrews University, he was a co-founder of the Early Music Society and performed in concerts with the Renaissance Group of St Andrews on tours of Europe and East Anglia. He has worked for a time as a digital recording editor with the BMP The Sound Recording Company, who were and are still responsible for recordings of Examination syllabus instrumental music for the Associated Board.

Although much of his career has been spent outside music, he keeps his hand in as an amateur musician for pleasure. As well as his first love, Early Music, he also enjoys Classical Music, Jazz, Folk rock and electronic music, and will listen to just about anything and play in any style.

Contents

	Title	Composer Publisher
1	Pavane Bittre Reue (Mille Regretz)	Susato
2	Basse Dance 1 (Erset Tanzbuch 1530)	Attaignant
3	Gaillarde Traditore	Phalese
4	Schafertanz Ohne Fels (Bergeret Sans Roch)	Susato
5	Tedesca e Salterello	Mainerio
6	Bransle de Champaigne X, XI and Bransle III	Gervaise
7	Volta CCX, CCXI, CCI	Praetorius
8	Putta Nera (Ballo Furlano)	Phalese
9	Narrenaufzug (Parade de Bouffons)	Susato
10	Pass'emezzo della Paganina	Phalese
11	Schafertanz	Susato
12	Laroque Gaillarde	Phalese
13	Bransle de La Torche	Praetorius
14	Gaillarde d'Ecosse	Phalese
15	Allemande No 1	Susato
16	Ballet CCLXVIII	Praetorius
17	Je Ne Fus Jamais Si Aise	Pierre Certon
18	Dindirin, Dindirin	Anon Spanish
19	Pase El Agoa	Anon Spanish
20	Ronde Mein Freund (Mon Amy)	Susato
21	The Earl of Essex Galliard	Dowland
22	Helas Madame	Henry VIII

1. Pavane Bittre Reue (Mille Regretz)

Dansereye 1551

Tielman Susato

2. Basse Dance 1 (Erstes Tanzbuch 1530)

Pierre Attaignant

3. Gaillarde Traditore
1571 Antwerp

Pierre Phalese

4. Schafertanz Ohne Fels (Bergerette Sans Roch)

Dansereye 1551 — Tielman Susato

2
33 C C F C G Dm G Dm G C F G C C
42 C F C G Dm C C B♭ C F G C C C F
51 C G Dm G Dm C F G C C C F C G
60 Dm C C B♭ C F G C

Nachtanz
3
65
C C F C B♭ F C Am Dm F G C
73
C G Dm E♭ D G Dm Dm C Dm B♭ A D
81
C G Dm E♭ D G C C B♭ C F G C
89
C C F C B♭ F C C B♭ C F G C

5. Tedesca e Salterello
Il Primo Libro de Balli (1578)

Giorgio Mainerio

2
37
Dm A Dm C F G C D G G Dm Dm A Dm A Dm C F Am B♭ A
44
Dm B♭ Gm Dm A Dm A Dm G F Gm Am B♭ A Dm C F Dm
51
Am A Gm C Gm F Dm C F G C D G G C
58
F Dm Am A Gm C Gm F Dm C F G C D G G

6. Bransle de Champaingne X, XI and Bransle III

Sixieme Livre de Danceries 1555, Troisieme Livre de Danceries 1557

Claude Gervaise

2
25
Gm Dm B♭ F B♭ Dm Am Dm Am D Gm Gm Dm B♭ F B♭ Cm F Gm
32
D Gm
Bransle III
G C G C G Am C G D G G G G Dm G
38
G C G C G Am C D D G G C G F G Am C G D G
44
G G G D G G C G F G Am C G D G

7. Volte CCX, CCXI, CCI

Terpsichore 1612

Michael Praetorius

Volte CCXI

Volte CCI

♩ = 120
D D G A D D Bm A D D G A D D A D D D A
10
G D D D G A Bm A D G A Bm Bm D A D D A D G Em D
19
A D D A D D G A D G A D G Em D A D D A D G G A D

8. Putta Nera (Ballo Furlano)

Pierre Phalese

9. Narrenaufzug (Parade des Bouffons)

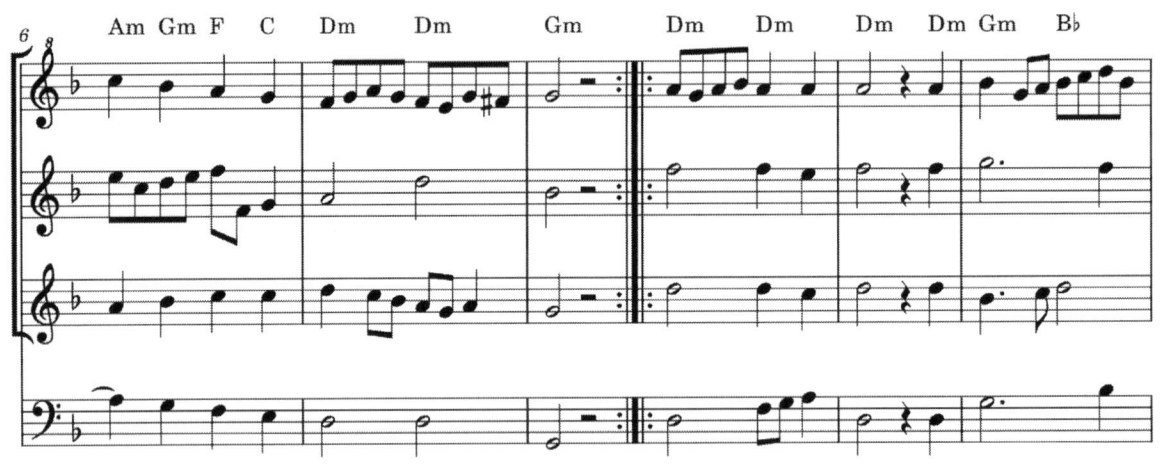

Dansereye 1551

Tielman Susato

2

F Bb F Eb C Dm Gm Gm Dm F F C
Dm Eb D Gm Gm C Gm F Bb F Eb C Dm Gm
Gm Dm F F F C Dm Cm D Gm

10. Pass'emezzo della Paganina

Anon Italian pub Phalese 1583

Maximilian with his musicians. From Der Weisskunig (1505-16)
Hans Burgkmair

11. Schäfertanz

Dansereye 1551

Tielman Susato

2
Fine
13
Dm C Dm G G A B♭ A B♭ A Dm G Dm
17
Dm C C F C F C C C G C
D.C. al Fine
21
C G Dm Am B♭ Am Em Am Dm G Dm G

12. Laroque Gaillarde

Pierre Phalese

2
22
Bb Eb Dm C F F F Bb C G C G F
29
F Dm Bb Gm Bb C C F F F Bb C
35
G C F F F Gm Bb Bb Gm C F

13. Bransle de La Torche

Terpsichore 1612

Michael Praetorius

14. Gaillarde d'Ecosse

Pierre Phalese 1571

15. Allemande No 1
Dansereye 1551

Tielman Susato

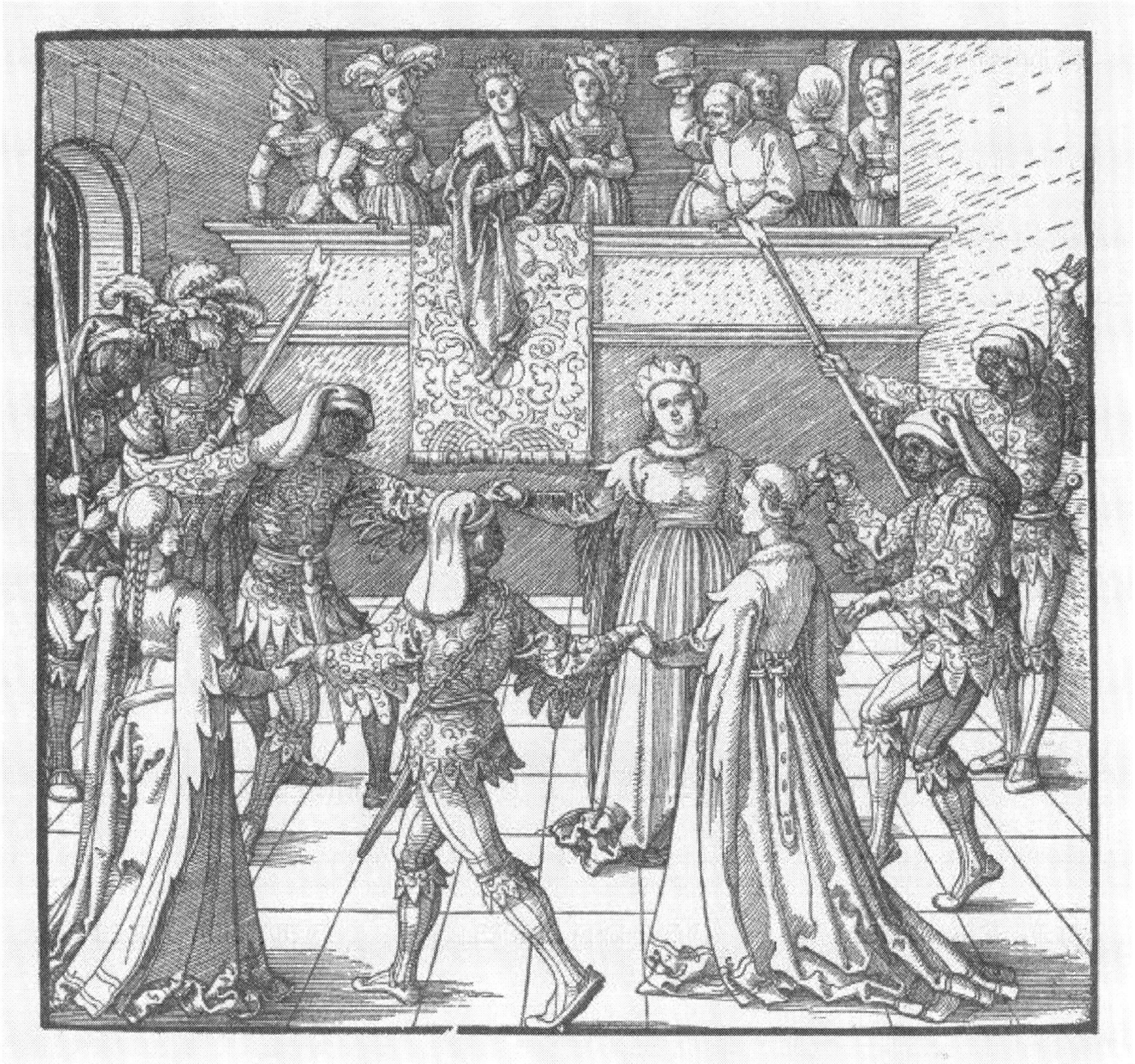

16. Ballet CCLXVIII
Terpsichore 1612

Michael Praetorius

2
18
B♭ Gm B♭ F Gm B♭ Gm D B♭ Gm B♭ F
24
Gm Cm Dm G Gm B♭ F Gm D
30
B♭ F Gm Cm D G G
D.C. al Fine

17. Je Ne Fus Jamais Si Aise

Piere Certon

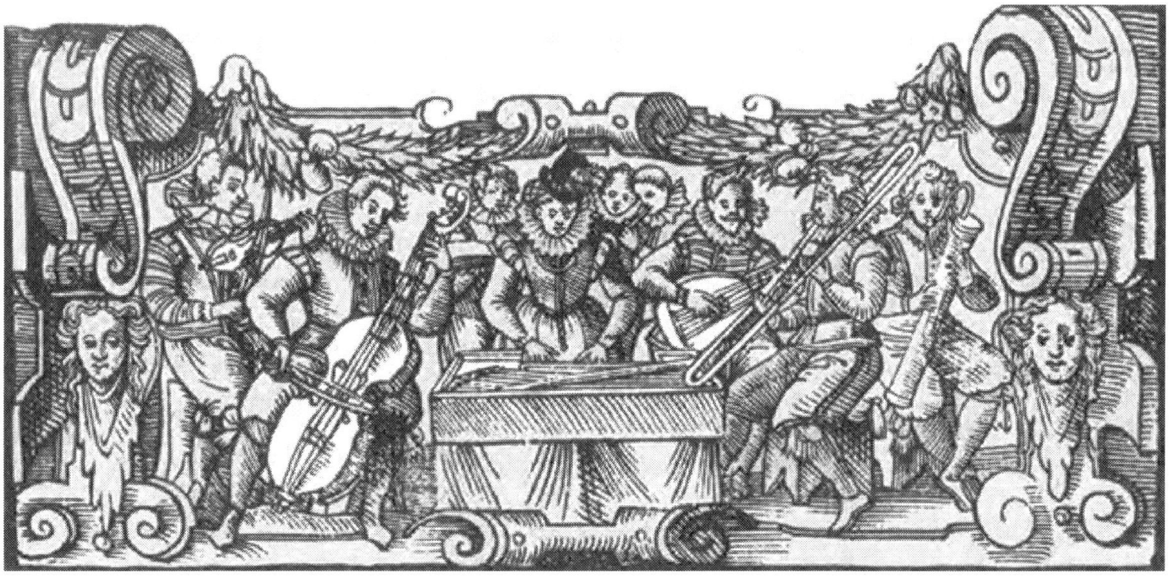

18. Dindirin, Dindirin
El Cancionero de Palacio (1474-1516)

Anon Spanish.

19. Pase El Agoa

El Cancionero de Palacio (1474-1516)

Anon Spanish.

20. Ronde Mein Freund (Mon Amy)
Dansereye 1551

Tielman Susato

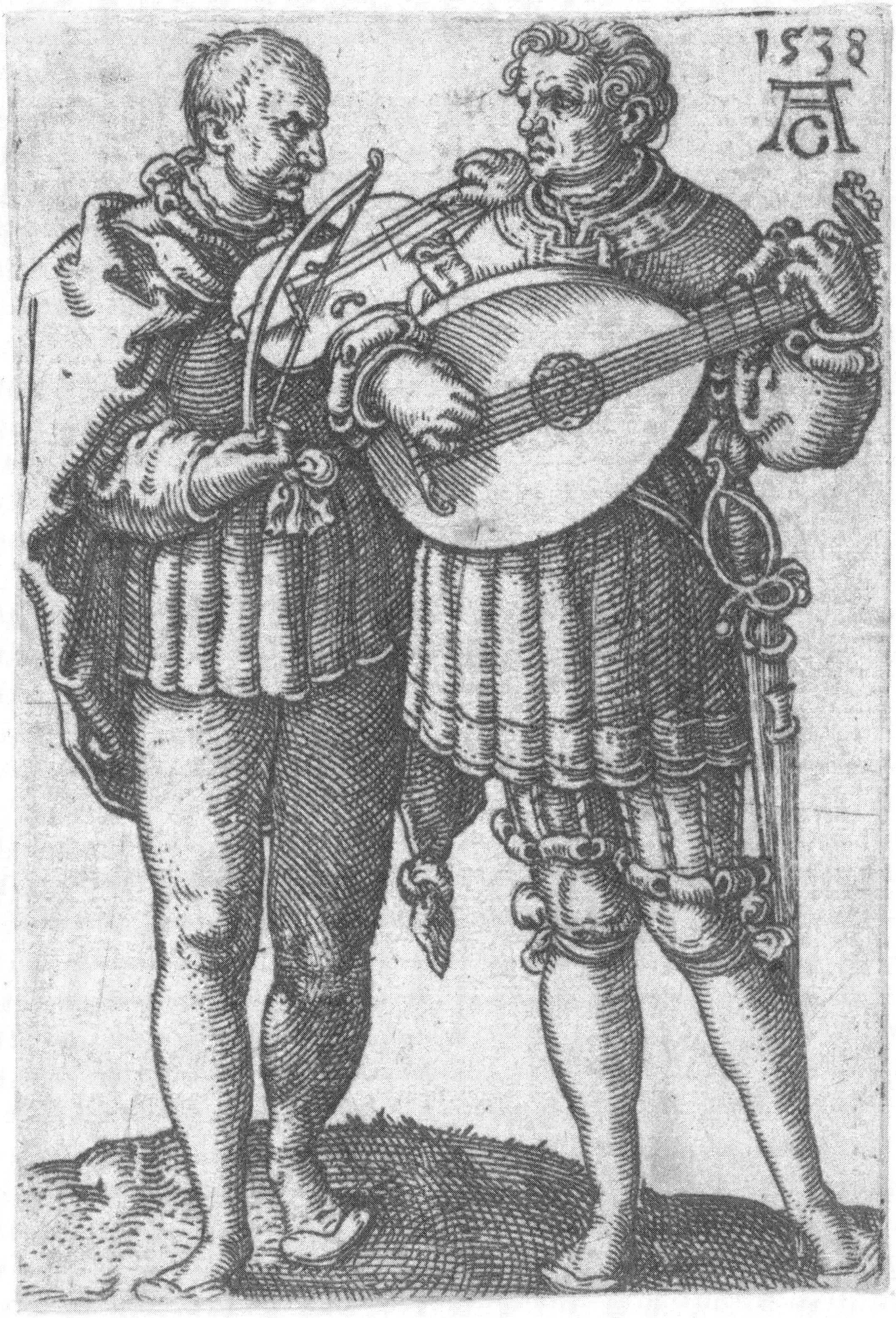
1538

21. The Earl of Essex Galliard

London 1605

John Dowland

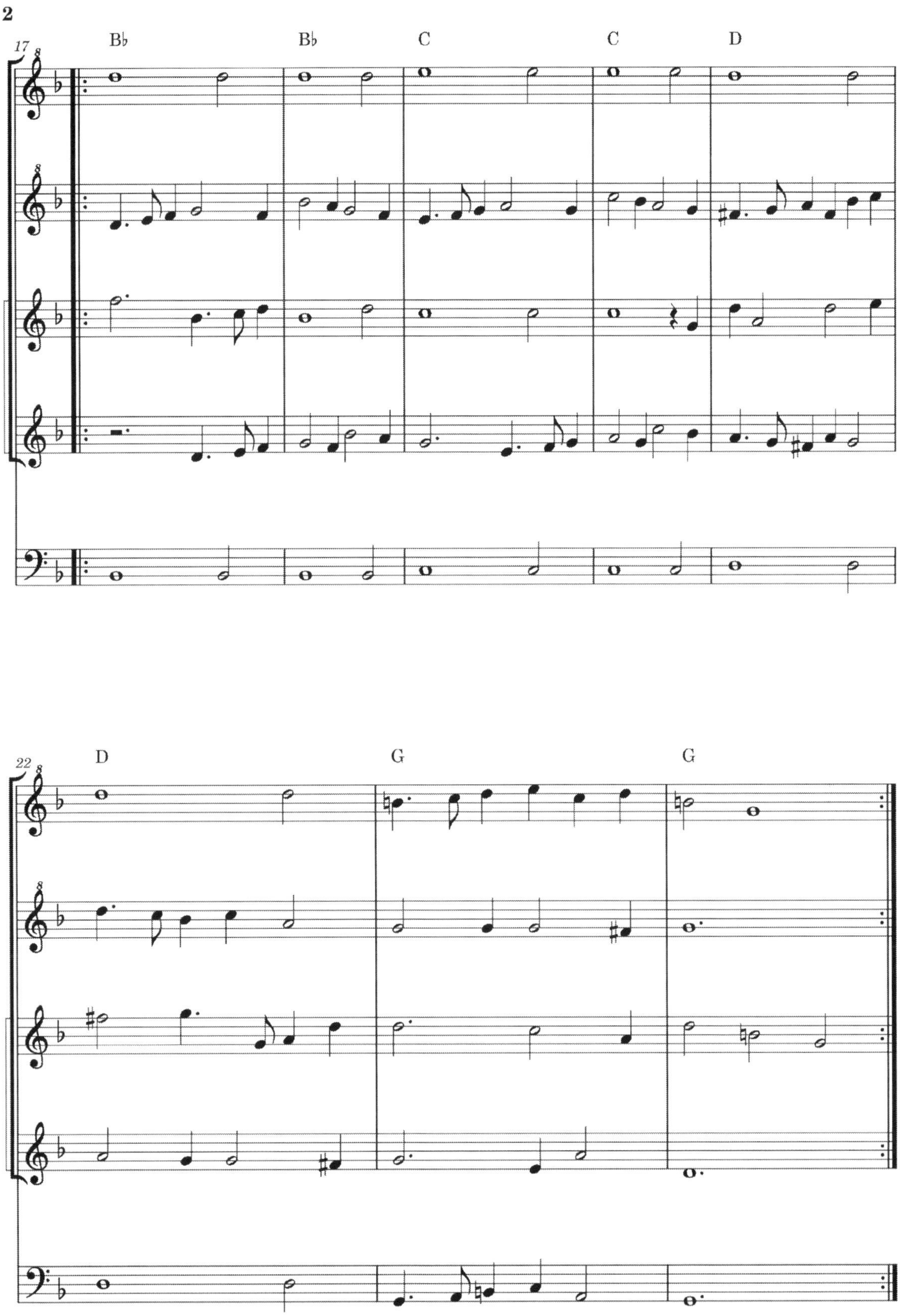
2
17
B♭
B♭
C
C
D
22
D
G
G

22. Helas Madame

from Henry VIII Songbook

Notes

1   Pavane Bittre Reue (Mille Regretz)   Susato

Dansereye was a volume published in 1551 in Antwerp by Tielman Susato. We know little about Susato, but his name may suggest he came from Soest.

The printing press and new technologies were making it easier and cheaper to spread music throughout Europe and Tielman Susato's press "At the Sign of the Crumhorn" was turning out chansons motets and masses, both composed by himself and others. Dansereye was produced for dance consorts and although no specific instruments are mentioned, the four parts are arranged for choirs of instruments, and are often suitable for the restricted range of woodwind instruments of the day, such as the crumhorn of his sign. Mille Regretz is not a composition by Susato, but a very popular chanson which was known elsewhere.

Mile regretz de vous abandonner
Et d'eslonger vostre fache amoureuse,
Jay si grand deuil et paine douloureuse,
Quon me verra brief mes jours definer.

A thousand regrets at deserting you
And leaving behind your loving face,
I feel so much sadness and such painful distress,
That it seems to me my days will soon dwindle away.

A version was certainly made by Josquin des Prez (1450/5-1521) and he may well have been the original composer.

2   Basse Dance 1 (Erset Tanzbuch 1530)   Attaignant

Pierre Attaignant (1494-1551 or 1552) was a pioneer of printing music by movable type which made it more affordable. He worked in Paris in workshops around the Sorbonne. Attaignant published over 1500 chansons by many different composers, including Claudin de Sermisy, Pierre Sandrin, Pierre Certon, Clement Janequin and five books of chansons by Josquin Desprez. Attaignant was named printer and bookseller for Music to the King of France (Francois I). By the time he published this in 1530, the Basse Dance was quite an old fashioned dance, so called because it was quite stately and feet were kept close to the floor. This one is scored in five parts.

3   Gaillarde Traditore   Phalese

Pierre Phalese the Younger (1545-1629) worked with his father Pierre Phalese as a printer and publisher in his native Leuven and then later in Antwerp. He was born Pieter van der Phaliesen and like many renaissance writers, often used a Latinisation of his name, Petrus Phalesius. He copied many sources in his publishing, and this tune also appears in a simplified form in the dancing manual "Orchesographie" by Thoinot Arbeau. Arbeau says he first heard it when he was learning to dance in Poitiers. This shows how fluidly these tunes were transmitted across Europe. The original was, it seems, an older Italian song. A Gaillarde or Galliard often the companion of a Pavan and is a more lively dance which involves kicking steps.

4   Schafertanz Ohne Fels (Bergeret Sans Roch)   Susato

A Schafertanz or Bergeret is a shepherd tune or dance, and shows how many of the melodies were collected from rustic folk originals and passed on by the dancing masters and adopted by more high art composers as a form in itself. People in court often hankered for the simplicity of pastoral scenes and this is reflected in contemporary paintings and tapestries. At the end of the dance is a Nachtantz - just as you get to the end of the dance and you are totally Nacht the band keeps going!

5   Tedesca e Salterello   Mainerio

Il Primo Libro De Balli was published in Venice by Giorgio Mainerio in 1578. He was born in Parma, Italy somewhere between 1530 and 1540 and died in Venice in 1582. Mainerio often signed his name Mayner from which some have suggested that his father was Scottish. A Tedesca is a German dance, and a Saltarello is almost the opposite of a Basse Dance being a jumping dance of mediaeval origin

6   Bransle de Champaigne X, XI and Bransle III   Gervaise

Claude Gervaise (1525-1583) was Attaignant's assistant and he continued the printing business with his widow. He published six books of Danceries. A Bransle, also known as Branle, Brangle or Brawl is a dance step and a dance in itself and gets its name from its swaying sideways motion. Gervaise has them as simple double or gay or from various locales- Picardie, Poictou, Bourgogne Champaigne. These seem to have been genuinely rural dances which had been collected and were being adopted by the courts. We are fortunate to have Arbeau's Orchesographie published in 1589, which is a manual which describes the steps of the bransles of Poitou, Bourgogne and Champagne. Arbeau also describes the bransles of the Haut Barrois, the Montardon, the Maltese, the Scottish and Trihory. Four others, Lyon, Hainault, Camp and Avignon are referred to without instructions. The bransles lend themselves to being combined into suites or sets in much the same way as happens today with Scottish, Irish or English country dance tunes.

7   Volta CCX, CCXI, CCI   Praetorius

Michael Praetorius lived between 1571 and 1617) Praetorius' German name was Michael Schultze. He was born in 1571 in Creuzburg in Thuringia, the son of a Lutheran Pastor. Praetorius was Organist and Kapellmeister to Henry Julius, Duke of Brunswick-Luneburg, and after 1613 he also began working at the court of John George I, Elector of Saxony at Dresden. As well as being a notable German renaissance composer and music publisher, Praetorius is important to us as a musicologist whose work Syntagma Musicum gives us scaled drawings and descriptions of the instruments of the times. Terpsichore is a publication of some 400 courtly dances. Some of the tunes were collected by Francis Caroubel, a french court violinist, whilst other works are Praetorius' own or from other sources. All three of these voltas are credited to MPC which in his edition denotes his own composition (Michael Praetorius of Creuzberg).

The Volta involves the propulsion of the females through the air by the males by means that were considered somewhat scandalous at the time. Arbeau in his Orchesographie says the fault lies more with the dancers than the dance itself;
"Nowadays, dancers lack these courteous considerations in their lavoltas and other similarly wanton and wayward dances that have been brought into usage. In dancing them the damsels are made to bounce about in such a fashion that more often than not they show their bare knees unless they keep one hand on their skirts to prevent it"
"This manner of dancing seems neither beautiful nor honourable to me unless one is dancing with some strapping hussy from the servants' hall"

8   Putta Nera (Ballo Furlano)   Phalese

Pierre Phalese published this tune in 1583 in Antwerp in his "Recueil de danseries, contenant presque toutes sortes de dances" but he was quite notorious for lifting arrangements from works published by others. The dance also appears in exactly the same form in Giorgio Mainerio's Il Primo Libro di Bali published in Venice in 1578. One could say that at least Phalese was disseminating the music 1200 kilometres away from its original publication. A Furlano is a dance from the Friuli region of Northern Italy. A politically correct translation for Putta Nera would probably be a sex worker of African Heritage.

9   Narrenaufzug (Parade de Bouffons, Entré du fol)   Susato

A very suitable entrance piece for early musicians, since most of us are mad. It is still quite a classy piece. Thoinot Arbeau has instructions for a dance called Buffens in his Orchesographie of 15 89 and although his tune is different from Susato's, it seems likely that Narrenaufzug was intended for much the same sort of dance.

"This is a silly dance. Think young buffoons showing off with a mock-serious sword dance.Think a feast of Fools. The amusement is greatly enhanced by the dancers, who have taken it upon themselves a pompous air, being well known to the crowd" Arbeau Orchesographie 1589

April fools day emerged out of Europe at this time, and the clergy were working on banning the remnants of the "Feast of Fools" (January 1st) of mediaeval times, on which a false Bishop, Archbishop or Pope would be elected by the lower clergy. Similarly, Plato's allegory of a Ship of Fools- a rudderless vessel crewed by incompetents was gaining favour amongst renaissance humanist thinkers. By the time of the reformation, this was no longer something to joke about.

10   Pass'emezzo della Paganina   Phalese

This is yet another example of a piece lifted directly from Mainerio. Phalese published this version in Antwerp in 1583, but it first appears in Giorgio Mainerio's Venetian publication, Il Primo Libro di Bali in 1578. A passamezzo, pass'emezzo or passe' mezzo is an Italian folk dance (a translation would be step and a half). This one comes from Paganina in the Veneto region.

11   Schafertanz   Susato

Another Schafertanz or shepherds dance. This one has a more plaintive melody that works well on Shawm or Rauschpfeife, and one can easily imagine an original played on bagpipes by a lone figure amongst the sheep.

12   Laroque Gaillarde   Phalese

This dance of Italian origin appears in various other sources and was something of a consort standard.

13   Bransle de La Torche   Praetorius

Although Bransle de La Torche is credited to Michael Praetorius of Creuzberg in the Terpsichore edition, this probably refers to the 5 part arrangement. And It includes a ground bass (or chord progression) known as the Passamezzo Antico that will appear in a great many tunes including the next one, the Galliarde d'Ecosse by Phalese.

The melody appears in Arbeau's Orchesographie as Branle de Chandelier with his dance instructions:

"This branle, otherwise called the branle de la torche, is danced to a medium binary measure, like and with the same steps as the Allemande. Whoever wants to dance, takes a candlestick with the lighted candle, or a torch or torch, and dancing and walking forward a turn or two around the hall, looking here and there at the one he wants to lead, chooses her as it seems to him, and dance together for a short space of time. and finally... making a bow, gives her the candlestick, torch or torch, and while dancing retires to her place. The young lady holding the candlestick does as she saw the young man do, and while dancing, goes to choose another, to whom finally, after having put him in his place, she gives the candlestick."

Praetorius's scoring favours an alto instrument on the top line, which may suggest he was envisioning a low consort of instruments descending to a Great Bass instrument on the bottom line. I have transposed the melody to favour a soprano or tenor instrument. This also brings it into the same key as the Gaillarde d'Ecosse, so that they will work as a pair together.

14   Gaillarde d'Ecosse   Phalese

Galliarde d'Ecosse pairs well with Bransle de La Torche as it is also based on the Passamezzo Antico, Unusually for Phalese, I have not found another version of the Gaillarde d'Ecosse, but Arbeau has a pair of Bransle d'Ecosse to unrelated tunes.   Scotland had cultural links with Europe through various dynastic marriages.

15   Allemande No 1   Susato

As the name suggests, the Allemande is a German dance, and Arbeau refers to it as an Alman. He says it it slow and sedate and "one of our oldest dances"

16   Ballet CCLXVIII   Praetorius

The term Ballet in Praetorius' time was used simply of a dance (as in the Italian Ballo) and not as a piece of dance performance that came to be popularised in France later in the century. Praetorius credits this Ballet as Incerti, which indicates it comes from an anonymous source.

For those of you interested in ornamentation, or "divisions" as they were known, Praetorius writes them into his part, so that we see the unadorned melody in the first eight bars, followed by a decorated version for the next eight bars. These ones are very restrained; skilled players of the renaissance would often demonstrate their virtuosity with even more wild flights of fancy.

17   Je Ne Fus Jamais Si Aise   Pierre Certon

This is actually a three part chanson written by the composer Pierre Certon who died in Paris in 1572 and was born some time between 1510 and 1520. He was master of Choristers at Saint Chapelle and was also Canon at the Cathedral at Melun. He served in the court to King Francis I.

"I never have enjoyed myself so much before as in these past three days: I have danced the time away to the sound of fifes and drums".

18	Dindirin, Dindirin	Anon Spanish
19	Pase El Agoa	Anon Spanish

Dindirin and Pase El Agoa are anonymous songs which come from the Cancionero de Palacio, a composite manuscript which was put together over the years 1474- 1517 for the Royal court of Madrid. The music was mainly collected under the patronage of Queen Isabella I of Castile and King Ferdinand II of Aragon whose marriage brought about the unification of Spain.

Dindirin is the onomatopoeic call of the nightingale- "Nightingale, oh Nightingale, do this errand for me, tell my lover that I am already married! Din-di-rin-din"

Pase el agoa is trying to encourage the young Julietta to "cross the water"- surely a euphemism.

20	Ronde Mein Freund (Mon Amy)	Susato

A ronde, ronde, rondel and rondelet also known as the carole was a simple mediaeval circular dance.

21	The Earl of Essex Galliard	Dowland

John Dowland (1563-1628) worked as a Lutenist to King Christian IV of Denmark and James I in England, and published music in London. The Earl of Essex Galliard was published in his "Lachrimæ or seaven teares figured in seaven passionate pavans, with divers other pavans, galliards and allemands, set forth for the lute, viols, or violons, in five parts" in 1604. The tunes may well have been of some age before publication, and this Galliard was dedicated to Robert Devereux, 2nd Earl of Essex a one time favourite of Elizabeth I. It appeared in Dowland's First Book of Songs (1597) as "Can she excuse my wrongs with vertues cloake". Possibly the dedication to the Earl of Essex Galliard suggests that the author of the poem was Devereux and Dowland composed the melody as a setting for it.

22	Helas Madame	Henry VIII

As we have seen with other pieces, authorship is always a complex problem. The melody to Helas Madame appears in a manuscript from Bayeaux from the end of the 15th Century. It seems quite possible that Henry could have composed the harmonies. The piece comes from the Henry VIII songbook which contains works by other composers as well as 30 or so works attributed to The Kinge H. VIII. Given the level to which Henry was educated, it is to be expected that he would have been a competent musician and composer.

The inventories show that he owned multiple bagpipes, clavichords, crumhorns, cornetts, instruments called 'dulcenses', flutes, fifes, gitteron pipes called cornets; a harpsichord, one regal, virginals; double virginal, double regal; lutes; gitteron (gittern), organs, portative organs; recorders; shawms; taberde and viols;

Printed in Great Britain
by Amazon